HURRICANE KATRINA
AND THE FLOODING OF
NEW ORLEANS

BY MARY K. PRATT

A CAUSE-AND-EFFECT
INVESTIGATION

CAUSE + EFFECT
DISASTERS

LERNER PUBLICATIONS ◆ MINNEAPOLIS

Lerner Publications Company
A division of Lerner Publishing Group, Inc.
241 First Avenue North
Minneapolis, MN 55401 USA

For reading levels and more information, look up this title at www.lernerbooks.com.

Content Consultant: Daniel P. Aldrich, Professor and Co-Director, Security and Resilience Studies Program, Northeastern University

Library of Congress Cataloging-in-Publication Data

The Cataloging-in-Publication Data for *Hurricane Katrina and the Flooding of New Orleans: A Cause-and-Effect Investigation* is on file at the Library of Congress.
ISBN 9781512411171 (lib. bdg.)
ISBN 9781512411287 (EB pdf)

Manufactured in the United States of America
1 - VP - 7/15/16

TABLE OF CONTENTS

A STORM OUT AT SEA

On August 24, 2005, people along the United States Gulf Coast woke up to another hot summer day. The Gulf Coast region borders the Gulf of Mexico, stretching from Texas through Louisiana, Mississippi, and Alabama to Florida's western coast. The Gulf Coast's beaches and other seaside attractions draw thousands of tourists each year. Many visit one of the country's most famous cities: New Orleans.

New Orleans is the largest city in Louisiana. For centuries, the region was home to American Indians. In 1541, explorer Hernando de Soto claimed the area for Spain. Then, in 1682, a French explorer, Robert de La Salle, claimed the Louisiana region for France. Soon after, settlers from Spain and France moved to the area. People from other European countries, including England and Germany, soon followed. People from Africa and the West Indies also arrived on the coast. Many were brought to the region as slaves. This early mix of cultures shaped modern New Orleans.

By the late 1800s, New Orleans was a bustling city. Steamboats carried goods and people down the Mississippi River to its busy seaport.

The residents of New Orleans are diverse. In the summer of 2005, about 484,000 people lived there. Many were descendants of French settlers. Others were descendants of the African American slaves and free blacks who had lived in the state. Others had Spanish or American Indian ancestors. New Orleans also had a large number of people living in poverty. The city's diverse mix of people created a unique culture. This gave the city its reputation for good food, great music, and colorful celebrations. The city's most famous slogan is *Laissez les bons temps rouler*. It means "Let the good times roll."

New Orleans is known for its architecture, which reflects a blend of influences.

Mardi Gras is a popular celebration in New Orleans featuring a big parade with colorful floats and costumes.

On August 23, 2005, the good times were about to be interrupted. The National Hurricane Center announced that it had spotted a tropical depression above the Atlantic Ocean. A tropical depression is a small storm. The storm hovered about 350 miles (563 kilometers) east of Florida. When a tropical depression gets stronger it becomes a tropical storm. When the winds of a tropical storm start moving at 74 miles (119 km) per hour or faster, the tropical storm becomes a hurricane.

By August 24, the tropical depression had become a tropical storm. The National Hurricane Center gave it the name Katrina. The storm moved westward across the Atlantic Ocean toward Florida, growing stronger. By the next day, it had developed into a Category One hurricane. Category One is the slowest and least destructive hurricane size. Category Five is the strongest and most dangerous.

Officials at the National Hurricane Center used computers to closely monitor Katrina as the storm grew stronger.

Hurricane Katrina hit southern Florida on August 25. The storm blew over trees, which killed two people. It damaged several buildings. But it wasn't a very strong storm.

Next, Katrina continued to travel west. It headed out over the Gulf of Mexico. Katrina had weakened crossing Florida. It was now just a tropical storm. But the Gulf of Mexico's warm water made Katrina stronger again, turning it back into a hurricane.

Katrina became a Category Three hurricane on August 27 as it traveled over the Gulf of Mexico. And this time, it kept getting stronger. By 2:00 a.m. on August 28, Katrina was a Category Four hurricane. Its winds were whipping at 145 miles (233 km) per hour. It now had the potential to cause a lot of damage if it made landfall. And it looked like the storm was going to turn north—headed straight into New Orleans.

Hurricane Katrina inches closer to New Orleans.

At 9:30 a.m. on August 28, New Orleans mayor Ray Nagin ordered a mandatory evacuation. That meant everyone had to leave the city. People needed to find safe shelter in regions far away from the Gulf Coast.

It seemed like the evacuation order came just in time. Katrina became a Category Five hurricane less than two hours later. Its strongest winds were blowing at 175 miles (282 km) per hour. It was one of the most powerful hurricanes ever recorded.

Officials at the National Hurricane Center warned that the hurricane could cause catastrophic damage. New Orleans was in particular danger. A rise of ocean water caused by the hurricane, called a storm surge, could crash over the city's levees. The levees separated the city from rivers, lakes, and canals. They helped protect the city and other parts of Louisiana from flooding. But now many officials and residents nervously wondered whether the levees would withstand Katrina.

Residents leaving New Orleans after the evacuation order wait in an enormous traffic jam.

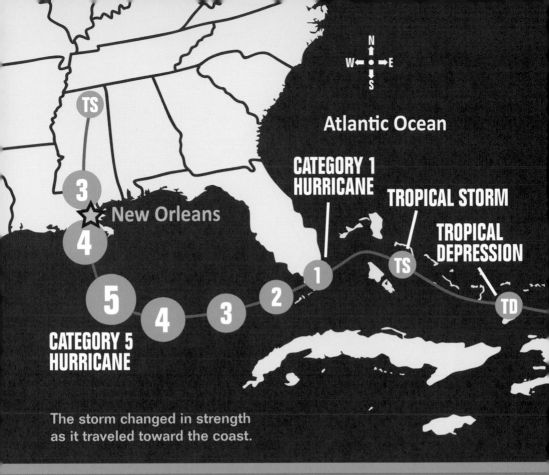

The storm changed in strength as it traveled toward the coast.

Hundreds of thousands of people from New Orleans and other parts of Louisiana drove away from the danger. But about one hundred thousand people stayed in New Orleans. Many could not leave because they did not have cars or enough money for transportation.

Mayor Nagin opened the Louisiana Superdome, a sports stadium in New Orleans. He called it a "shelter of last resort" for people who could not leave the city. About ten thousand of the remaining New Orleans residents went to the Superdome.

As the storm approached, everyone left in New Orleans hunkered down. People around the country watched television coverage to see what would happen. Everyone wondered: How bad would the damage be?

THE STORM STRIKES

The residents of New Orleans and
the rest of the Gulf Coast region
had good reason to be worried about
Hurricane Katrina. Past hurricanes had
devastated the area. During the twentieth century alone, six
hurricanes had left New Orleans flooded with water. Hurricanes
are particularly devastating to New Orleans because of the
city's geography. New Orleans sits between two large bodies of
water—the Mississippi River and Lake Pontchartrain. This made
the city prone to flooding during heavy rains and storms.

The Causeway Bridge runs
across Lake Pontchartrain,
toward New Orleans.

This 1910 photograph shows one of the many artificial canals in New Orleans.

In the nineteenth century, civic leaders built pumps and canals to drain water out of the region. This created more dry land for people to build on. But the drained land was actually 7 to 10 feet (2 to 3 meters) below sea level. As a result, New Orleans is like a bowl that sits between two big bodies of water. The levees are like the sides of the bowl. They keep water from filling up New Orleans. Pumps and canals drain any water that does get in. The US Army Corps of Engineers (USACE) is in charge of building and maintaining the levees.

On August 29, the city braced for the worst as Katrina spun closer. The storm was heading just west of the city. That was the worst-case scenario because the strongest winds and biggest storm surge are on the east side of a storm. New Orleans would get the worst winds and water that the storm would produce.

Hurricane Katrina made landfall at 6:10 a.m. on August 29 as a Category Three hurricane. The storm was 400 miles (644 km) across. The winds whipped at upwards of 140 miles (225 km) per hour.

Katrina brought heavy rains and dangerously strong winds to New Orleans. As predicted, it also delivered huge storm surges. The storm surges overwhelmed the levees in and around New Orleans. They topped or breached levees in fifteen different spots. Water rushed into the city.

In one case, a 15-foot (4.6 m) wave traveled from the Gulf of Mexico straight up the Gulf Intercoastal Waterway, one of the many canals around New Orleans. The wave smashed into the Industrial Canal on New Orleans's eastern border. The water first went over

Water pours into the city through breached levees.

the top of the earthen levees around the canal. The force of the flood then scoured away the bottom part of the levees.

Water poured into several poor and working-class neighborhoods. Those neighborhoods were New Orleans East, the Lower Ninth Ward, and the Upper Ninth Ward. St. Bernard Parish, a suburban and rural district next to New Orleans, was also flooded. The floodwaters reached into the wealthier Lakeview neighborhood, too.

Water filled buildings within minutes. Many people died trying to escape. Some ended up trapped on their roofs or in their attics in the middle of the storm. Others swam for their lives in floodwaters filled with dangers, such as debris, sewage, and poisonous snakes.

Two young people seek shelter in a doorway as Hurricane Katrina makes landfall in New Orleans on August 29.

High water broke through levees in three locations along canals north of the city, too. The London Avenue and 17th Street canals usually carried water out of New Orleans to the massive Lake Pontchartrain. But the breaches in these canals allowed water from the lake to pour back into the city.

The breaches happened while the hurricane was still striking New Orleans. The storm also knocked out electricity in the city. It took out telephone lines and cell phone communication.

By 2:00 p.m. on August 29, officials with the USACE checked on the levees. They could not reach the levees with their vehicles

EVACUATION ROUTE

because of the flooding and debris. But they knew that levees had failed because of the amount of flooding. The city's pumps and canals weren't powerful enough to handle the flood. And because they couldn't reach the levee breaches, they couldn't quickly plug them. Water continued to rush in.

Hurricane Katrina moved farther inland by early afternoon. It weakened as it moved away from New Orleans and the Gulf Coast. But its effects on the city continued. At nightfall, telephones and electricity remained out. People trapped in the dark, flooded city waited for help to arrive.

Stormwaters flooded entire neighborhoods. But since phone communication and electricity were out, many residents and government officials did not hear about the flooding right away.

THE STORM'S AFTERMATH

Katrina moved north into Tennessee by August 30. It had lost some strength. The storm was downgraded from a hurricane to a tropical storm. But New Orleans and the people there continued to suffer.

Multiple breaches continued to let water into the city. Seventy-five percent of New Orleans was flooded. Many people were trapped inside their houses in the heat and humidity that followed the storm. Some were stuck on their roofs or in trees. They desperately waited for rescuers to arrive. Others waded, swam, or floated in boats or on debris through the polluted floodwaters. They searched for dry ground.

New Orleans resident Terri Jones tries to cool down an overheated woman outside the Superdome on September 1.

Stephen Carter helps his daughter to safety as they are rescued from their flooded home in New Orleans on August 30.

Hundreds of people who had escaped the floodwaters waited on dry highway overpasses. They had little or no food and water. Many also had no shelter from the weather. They faced heat during the day and chilly air at night. They suffered bites from the bugs that swarmed the flooded city. They waited hours, or even days, for rescue workers to reach them.

This graphic shows the depth of the flooding in New Orleans on September 3.

Depth in feet
- 0-1
- 1-2
- 3-4
- 4-5
- 5-6
- 6-7
- 7-8
- 8-9
- 9-10
- 10-15
- 15-20
- 15-20
- >20

NOAA
NATIONAL OCEANIC AND ATMOSPHERIC ADMINISTRATION
U.S. DEPARTMENT OF COMMERCE

USACE Flood Status Zones

Zone ID

The Superdome was meant to be a safe place for people who hadn't left the city. But the conditions there were awful. About fifteen thousand people arrived at the Superdome after the storm, joining the ten thousand already there. Thousands of other stranded residents broke into the city's Ernest N. Morial Convention Center complex. They hoped to find a safe shelter where they could get food, medical help, and other necessities.

Neither location had enough supplies. There weren't enough workers, medicine, or food, or even basic supplies such as toilet paper. There was no running water or electricity after the storm, either.

Winds of up to 90 miles (145 km) per hour damaged the roof of the Superdome during the storm.

New Orleans became more dangerous in the hours and days after the storm. Some residents started taking things from unattended stores. Some people took supplies they needed to survive, such as food and water. But others looted whatever they could find, including expensive electronics and cars.

There were conflicts among the survivors as well. Police officials in at least one suburban community next to New Orleans refused to help people coming from the flooded city. Many said racism played a role in that incident. People in the suburb were mostly white. Hurricane survivors coming from New Orleans were mostly black.

Government officials worked to organize rescue workers and gather enough supplies to help. But it took a long time.

At first, officials did not know how big the problem was. It wasn't clear how many people needed help. The Federal Emergency Management Agency (FEMA) took days to organize rescue efforts. So did other federal, state, and local government agencies that are supposed to help in disasters.

People trapped by floodwaters try to get to higher ground on August 30.

By the time the water was pumped out of the city, many homes and buildings had been damaged beyond repair.

A US Coast Guard helicopter rescues a resident from his rooftop.

Eventually, help did come. The Coast Guard rescued about thirty-four thousand people in New Orleans. Citizens from around Louisiana and other states came in their own boats to rescue people. Others from around the country offered food and shelter.

Meanwhile, workers with the USACE continued to have trouble handling the breaches. The workers still could not drive their vehicles to the breaches because of the floodwaters and other damage. Instead, they used helicopters to drop sandbags into the holes in the levees. They eventually filled the breaks and pumped the water out of the city. But it took more than a month before New Orleans was dry. By then, the damage had been done.

Sheila Dixon
of the Gentilly
neighborhood in
New Orleans cries
after being airlifted
out of flooded
New Orleans on
August 31. She
lost her home
and had no idea
where she and
her family would
end up.

AN UNNATURAL DISASTER

Leaders with the National Guard had activated troops in the Gulf Coast region before Katrina hit so they could be ready to help after the storm. On September 2, more than thirty thousand National Guard troops started arriving in New Orleans. The troops helped search for victims and stranded survivors. They rescued people and treated injured residents. They carried food and water to those stranded in the city. Many relief organizations helped out, too. They relocated some survivors to other parts of Louisiana and in other states around the country.

A National Guard truck drives through floodwaters, bringing supplies to the Superdome.

Experts estimated that the storm caused between $100 and $200 billion in damage. About eighteen hundred people on the Gulf Coast died. About eight hundred thousand were left homeless. Many of those who died in New Orleans were elderly, sick, or poor. These people had trouble fleeing the storm. About sixty thousand houses were too damaged to repair.

Katrina's impact on New Orleans lasted a long time. Even ten years after the storm, the city had not fully recovered. Several neighborhoods, including the Lower Ninth Ward, still had abandoned and destroyed property. Many of the people who fled before the storm or were evacuated afterward stayed away from New Orleans. Some of them had no safe place to return to. Others did not want to come back. Others could not afford to rebuild their homes. Some of the survivors felt anxious and depressed. Many feared the possibility of another storm.

As New Orleans started to recover, the country had the chance to study the disaster. Kathleen Blanco, the governor of Louisiana when Katrina struck, said a few weeks after the storm, "We must take a careful look at what went wrong and make sure it never happens again." The hurricane itself was a natural occurrence. But it became clear that the tragedy that unfolded in New Orleans after the storm was an unnatural disaster.

About 20 percent of New Orleans residents did not leave before the storm. Experts estimated that about 112,000 New Orleans residents did not have access to cars. Without cars, it was difficult to leave. The city did not have good plans to help those who could not leave on their own.

In some areas, the floodwaters washed away entire homes and neighborhoods.

Some felt that racism played a part in the government's response. Most of the people who didn't evacuate were black. Many of them were poor. This limited their options for evacuation. Therefore, most of those who died during the storm or were stranded in flooded areas were black. Many said the government did not make saving these people a high priority.

Some of New Orleans's measures to keep water out of the city actually made the disaster worse. The canals allowed the storm surge to travel directly into the heart of the city. The levees, too, caused problems. After the storm, the USACE admitted the levees were not built or maintained correctly. There were problems with the sheet piling. These were the metal planks driven into the ground to make the levees stronger. The USACE said the piling did not go deep enough into the ground. The dirt used to build up the levees was also unstable. The soil shifted and eroded. This weakened the levees. Investigations also found that some government officials misspent government money that was supposed to pay for work on the levees.

Researchers also believed that keeping the Mississippi River from naturally flooding every year added to the disaster. Wetlands can soak up storm surges. But the canals and pumps had stopped the natural cycle. Without the silt from regular flooding, the Louisiana wetlands were shrinking. They were disappearing at a rate of 20 square miles (52 square kilometers) a year.

Volunteer construction workers with Habitat for Humanity help build new homes in the Upper Ninth Ward in August 2006.

Many government officials also botched their rescue work. Some agencies made their workers sit through training sessions in the days after Katrina hit instead of going to New Orleans to help. Some agencies, including the National Guard, did not send the right equipment or enough people with the right skills, such as medical training, to help with rescue efforts.

In the years following the storm, government leaders proposed changes to help prevent another disaster like Katrina. The federal government promised to spend $14.5 billion on new projects designed to prevent flooding in New Orleans and other places along the Mississippi River.

Other leaders proposed ideas to keep people safe from future storms. Some said the government should take away levees on parts of the Mississippi River. This would allow the river to run freely again. It would flood and deposit silt that would rebuild lost wetlands.

Many others suggested that the government restore the state's coastal marshlands. The state of Louisiana set up the Coastal Protection and Restoration Authority to work on this. The work would help reduce storm surges and the force of winds coming from the Gulf of Mexico. Some officials believe this is the best way to keep the city safe from the next monster hurricane, but more than a decade after Katrina, the project is still a work in progress.

Hurricane Katrina drastically changed New Orleans. It is no longer the city it once was. Some people left and never returned. Billions of dollars have been spent to rebuild, yet some damaged neighborhoods have not yet been fully rebuilt. Slowly, the city is reviving. Tourists are coming back, and the characteristics that made New Orleans unique—the food, the culture, the music— remain intact.

Six months after the hurricane, residents gather for a Mardi Gras parade.

CAUSE

In the nineteenth century, civic leaders drained land in New Orleans to create more space for people to build on.

Canals and pumps stopped the natural cycle of flooding in New Orleans.

Many people did not own cars or have the means to pay for transportation to evacuate the city before the hurricane hit.

Canals were built to keep water from flooding New Orleans.

USACE did not properly build or maintain the levees surrounding New Orleans.

EFFECT

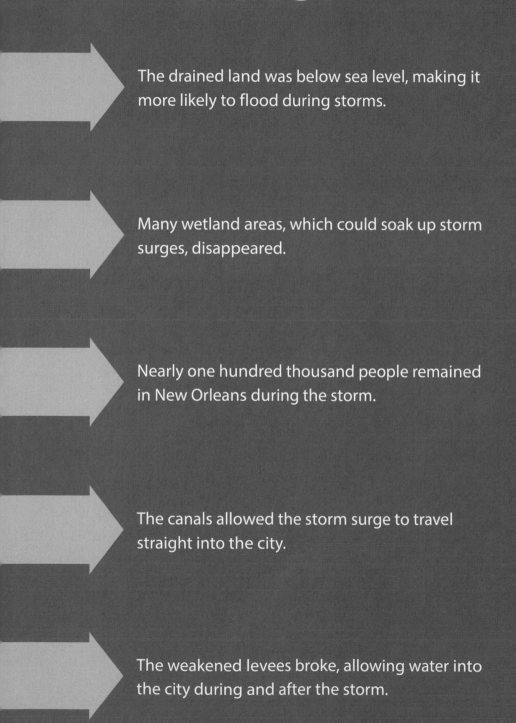

The drained land was below sea level, making it more likely to flood during storms.

Many wetland areas, which could soak up storm surges, disappeared.

Nearly one hundred thousand people remained in New Orleans during the storm.

The canals allowed the storm surge to travel straight into the city.

The weakened levees broke, allowing water into the city during and after the storm.

Glossary

attraction: an interesting thing or place that draws visitors

breach: a break, a hole, or an opening

canal: a human-made waterway

catastrophic: causing great damage or harm

debris: fragments of wreckage scattered around after a disaster

levee: an embankment, or mound, rising up and along a body of water to prevent flooding

loot: to steal or take

overpass: a road that passes over another road as a bridge

scour: to rub hard, or to remove by rubbing or washing

sea level: the level of the surface of the sea

sewage: wastewater and waste matter carried off in sewers

withstand: to hold up against

Source Notes

11 "Hurricane Katrina: 10 Years Later," *History,* accessed February 22, 2015, http://www.history.com/topics/hurricane-katrina.

30 "Looking Back: Quotes from Hurricane Katrina," *USA Today*, August 25, 2015, http://www.usatoday.com/story/news/nation-now/2015/08/21/looking-back-quotes-hurricane-katrina/31911813.

Selected Bibliography

Brinkley, Douglas. *The Great Deluge: Hurricane Katrina*. New York: Morrow, 2006.

Dryre, Willie. "Hurricane Katrina: The Essential Timeline." *National Geographic News*. November 24, 2015. http://news.nationalgeographic.com/news/2005/09/0914_050914_katrina_timeline.html

Horne, Jed. *Breach of Faith: Hurricane Katrina and the Near Death of a Great American City*. New York: Random House, 2006.

Kahn, Carrie. "New Orleans Police Struggle in Post-Katrina Era." *National Public Radio*. November 25, 2015. http://www.npr.org/templates/story/story.php?storyId=129090179

Powell, Lawrence N. *The Accidental City: Improvising New Orleans*. Cambridge, MA: Harvard University Press, 2012.

Further Information

Books

Brown, Don. *Drowned City: Hurricane Katrina and New Orleans*. New York: Houghton Mifflin Harcourt, 2015. This as-it-happens narrative tells the story of Hurricane Katrina and its aftermath.

Koontz, Robin. *What Was Hurricane Katrina?* New York: Grosset & Dunlap, 2015. Learn more about Hurricane Katrina's impact on New Orleans and other coastal communities.

Lusted, Marcia Amidon. *Surviving Natural Disasters*. Minneapolis: Lerner Publications, 2014. Read about survivors of natural disasters like Hurricane Katrina.

Websites

Live Science: Hurricane Katrina
http://www.livescience.com/22522-hurricane-katrina-facts.html
Learn more about Katrina's impact on New Orleans.

National Geographic: Katrina Extreme
http://video.nationalgeographic.com/video/news/katrina-mississippi-destruction-vin
See images of Hurricane Katrina's landfall on the Gulf Coast.

Time: Hurricane Katrina by the Numbers
http://time.com/4007368/hurricane-katrina-by-the-numbers-10-years-later
Take a look back at the disaster on its tenth anniversary.

Index

Photo Credits